What Every Catholic Needs to Know About the Mass

A Parish Guide to Liturgy

Kevin McGloin

Resource Publications, Inc.
San Jose, California

Reprint Department
Resource Publications, Inc.
160 E. Virginia Street #290
San Jose, CA 95112-5876
(408) 286-8505 (voice)
(408) 287-8748 (fax)

Library of Congress Cataloging-in-Publication Data
McGloin, Kevin, 1959-
  What every Catholic needs to know about the Mass: a parish guide to liturgy / Kevin McGloin.
    p.   cm.
  Includes bibliographical references.
  ISBN 0-89390-536-4
  1. Mass 2. Lord's Supper—Catholic Church. 3. Catholic Church—Liturgy. I. Title.
BX2230.2 .M283 2001
264'.0203—dc21   2001019721

Printed in the United States of America.
07 08 09 10 11 | 5 4 3 2

Editorial director: Nick Wagner
Production: Romina Saha
Copyeditor: Robin Witkin
Cover design: Nelson Estarija

Contents

5

6

The History of the Liturgy

What we call the Last Supper was never named that by Jesus. "Do this as a remembrance of me" (Luke 22:19) was the phrase the Gospels used for the first Eucharist, which took place on the eve of Christ's passion. At that meal, Jesus took bread in his hands and it became his Body. He took a cup of wine in his hands and the wine became his Blood. Jesus then invited his disciples to eat his Body and drink his Blood.

Jesus did not pass down a literal transcript of what he said; we do not know the exact words he spoke at the Last Supper. He did not have a secretary on hand taking notes. Written approximately twenty years after the Last Supper, the first description the church has of Christ's words is found in 1 Corinthians 11.

The words "THIS IS MY BODY" and "THIS IS MY BLOOD" are found in the Gospels of Luke, Mark, and Matthew and the epistle of Paul. Scholars say that the statement is so brief and so striking that it is difficult to imagine that the phrases have undergone any change.

The four Gospels tell us that Jesus instituted the Eucharist. Paul's first letter to Corinth and the Book of Acts give us some picture of what the "breaking of the bread" was really like in the time of the apostles. This was an important period in the history of the Mass because such profound changes were made.

The Liturgy in the Apostolic Age

After Jesus died the apostles were troubled and confused. Their environment was so hostile that they feared for their lives. But with the coming of the Holy Spirit at Pentecost, the apostles were transformed. They regained their courage and began to go out in public to proclaim that Jesus was risen from the dead.

So what was the Mass like then? The apostles had Jesus' instruction: "Do this as a remembrance of me." But how were they to carry out this mandate?

How often would they celebrate it—once a year with Passover or more often? It would be a rite, but what would the ceremonial pattern be? These matters needed to be settled. Jesus had not given the church a ready-made eucharistic liturgy. The early church's task was to give the Mass form and expression in each ensuing age.

The apostles began their eucharistic worship by maintaining a liturgical bond with the Jewish temple. After returning home from the temple, the apostles would begin a second liturgy. In Acts 2:46, Luke writes: "They went to the temple area together everyday, while in their homes they broke bread." What today we refer to as the Old Testament was read in the temple, but the apostles celebrated the breaking of the bread in their homes. Scholars do not know how long the disciples celebrated the twofold liturgy, but their decision to break away from the temple seems to have been brought on by the Jewish leaders.

"The two basic elements of the Mass—the sacrifice and the gift of Christ as food—were undisputed realities for Christians in the Middle Ages. Theological reflection deepened and affirmed that in these two elements the whole Christ is present in the Body and Blood of Jesus in the Eucharist."

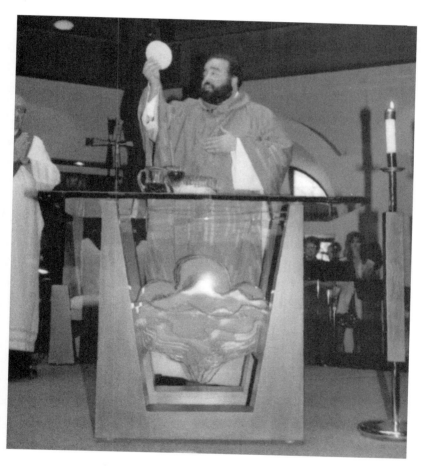

The Liturgy During a Time Of Torment

From 100 to 313 AD, the persecution of Christians forced the church to carry on a secret life. Each local church kept its own traditions, and the ability of members to travel between east and west enabled the churches to maintain communion with each other and with the Church of Rome. In addition to persecuting the Christians, enemies of the church spread lies about the nature of the ceremonies. For example, they claimed that Christians committed human sacrifice in their liturgy.

During this period Christians had what was called the "discipline of the secret," an early church practice of keeping liturgical mysteries a secret from those who were not baptized. Scholars believe one reason for this practice was that pagans accused Christians of cannibalism. This idea surely arose from the phrases "This is my Body" and "This is my Blood" used in the liturgical service.

Improvisation in the liturgy was the rule rather then the exception during this period, particularly in terms of the prayers of the Mass. Ancient documents show that presiders of the Eucharist were free, within limits, to compose their own prayers and organize the ritual. This improvisation did not allow the presider to say or do anything he wanted; he was still called to be faithful to the tradition of the church.

The introduction of Latin in the liturgy took place during this time because more people spoke Latin than Greek. This caused great tension among Greek-speaking Christians because Latin was considered a vulgar language spoken only by common people.

The presider was expected to wear his best clothes to celebrate the liturgy. There were no special vestments during this time.

The place where the celebrant sat or stood depended on the circumstance. When the Mass was celebrated within the context of a meal, the presider sat at the table with the people. If it was celebrated in a private home, the celebrant stood near the table surrounded by the people. When Mass was celebrated in a catacomb on the tomb of a martyr, the celebrant had his back to the people because these tombs were hollowed out of the walls.

The faithful shared communion standing up. They took the consecrated bread in their hands and drank the sacred wine from the chalice.

The Liturgy from Constantine To Gregory the Great

This age lasted from the time of the emperor Constantine's conversion in 313 AD until the death of St. Gregory the Great in 604 AD. When Constantine converted to Christianity, the church began to grow. Christians were no longer persecuted and soon Christianity became the privileged religion. No longer did Christians meet in private homes for Mass. The small groups had become large crowds. As great numbers of pagans converted to Christianity, Constantine gave their temples to the church. These long, narrow temples were used for Mass.

With so many people proclaiming to be followers of Christ, the church needed to establish order in the Mass. The Romans, who had a keen sense of order, procession, and pomp, did not take long to decide the exact roles played by the celebrant and the faithful. For many years, the precise order of the Mass was passed down from one master of ceremonies to the next by word of mouth and practice. Gradually the order of the Mass was put into writing.

The music during this period was exclusively vocal, because musical instruments were considered too tainted with paganism to be used in church. All of the chants were one-part singing.

The Liturgy During the Middle Ages

From 604 to 1517, many changes were made in the eucharistic liturgy. There were great processions and the papal Mass was filled with pomp and ceremony as dignitaries played solemn roles. The Mass was very formal and well organized.

People continued to receive communion under both forms, and the use of unleavened bread prevailed until the eleventh century. Soon the host became small, thin, round, and white. The size of the host made it difficult for people to receive it in their hands. It was judged to be more proper to receive it on the tongue. To receive communion on the tongue, it was easier for people to kneel, which was also a sign of respect. To make kneeling easier, an armrest was created—the communion rail. Little by little, new customs for the Mass came into being. Though none of the customs was from early church practice and none was Roman in origin, Rome later adopted them.

The separation of the presider from the people was stressed more and more. People went to communion less often. The altar was moved to the rear wall of the church. The priest turned around to face the altar, which meant his back was to the people. As a result, people could only see the priest off in the distance making mysterious gestures.

A great number of gestures were used during the Mass: signs of the cross, blessings, incensing, kissing of sacred objects, bows, genuflections. Because the people were no longer sharing in communion, elevating the consecrated host became a popular feature of the Mass. People just wanted to see the host, not receive it. Bells also came into use during this time. At first they were rung to call people to Mass. Eventually, however, mass servers at the foot of the altar used small bells to alert the faithful that the consecration was going to take place. The organ was also first used during this time; its origins can be traced to the East, not to Rome. Also the creed was introduced to the liturgy during the Middle Ages.

Scholars labeled the period from 1014 until 1517 the Gothic Mass. During this time little development occurred in the area of liturgy, while bold and creative changes took place in both theology and architecture. The liturgy took place amongst great pomp and pageantry in spectacular buildings that drew fascinated crowds. Gregorian music gave the church great works of music. Theologians and poets endowed the liturgy with beautiful hymns. But the liturgy was dissipating its strength on the excesses occurring during the Mass.

Professors of liturgy scrutinized the dogmatic rationale of the Mass with vigor, precision, and determination. Following the trend of popular piety, Gothic liturgists lost themselves in a cloud of rubrics and allegories. Meanwhile the liturgy did little more than give rise to popular devotions, some of which lapsed into deviations.

For the faithful, Low Masses became a popular devotion. People requested that Mass be celebrated for the deceased and for personal devotions because they were convinced of the value of the sacrifice of the Mass. What began to happen smacked of magic and superstition. People requested Masses based on the number of Masses said and on repetition. Some believed that if liturgies were said for the dead on several days in a row, their deceased loved ones would get into heaven more quickly.

The most important liturgy was the solemn High Mass, but the people or faithful (they were referred to as spectators) could only watch or observe the liturgy. They had no role. The priest read the epistle at the right side of the altar and the Gospel on the left side. This gave the spectators an idea of what part of the Mass the celebrant was at. Room was needed for the missal at both sides of the altar, so the altar had to be lengthened. Before this period, the altar had been approximately one square yard in size.

The two basic elements of the Mass—the sacrifice and the gift of Christ as food—were undisputed realities for Christians in the Middle Ages. Theological reflection deepened and affirmed that in these two elements the whole Christ is present in the Body and Blood of Jesus in the Eucharist. The people's desire to see the sacred species gave birth to the practice of elevating the host and chalice after the two consecrations at Mass. The people attached great importance to this gesture because it allowed them to see the host. The primary devotion for many people was the contemplation of the consecrated host during Mass. In cities people rushed from church to church to see the consecrated host as often as possible. At this time the people did not receive communion at Mass, only on their deathbed as Viaticum. They believed that seeing the host at Mass would bring them peace of mind.

In terms of singing, Gregorian chant was done only by the priest and the choir. The people had no part in it. The choir's role became more important and chants during the liturgy became more splendid. People went to church to hear the Mass. The organ played an increasing role in the Mass, as every large church had one. The priest's vestments and the altars became more ornate. Sculptures, statues, and paintings decorated the church. People may not have been able to understand what was taking place during the liturgy, but there was plenty to see.

The Liturgy and the Influences Of Luther and Trent

This era takes place from 1517 until the present day. Martin Luther had a tremendous impact on religion and civil affairs in the sixteenth century. According to Luther, the Mass was nothing more than superstition in the way it was celebrated and comprehended. Some members of the clergy were persuading the faithful (their fee providers) that "You never grow old during Mass," "You never fall ill at Mass," "Your deceased relatives in purgatory will have their suffering suspended during Mass," and so on.

Some reformers denied the real presence of Jesus in the Eucharist, but Luther believed in it. He did not believe in devotion to the real presence outside the celebration of the Last Supper.

Luther violently opposed the practice of Mass stipends, which some clergy and people abused.

Luther was an advocate of salvation by faith alone (*sola fides*). He wanted the preaching of the Word nourished by Scripture alone (*sola scriptura*) to have first place in the liturgy. Because baptism makes us a priestly people, Luther wanted the liturgy to be prayed and sung in German. In Germany this reformed worship became thoroughly German, and in Sweden it became Swedish. The same thing occurred in England and in France. In each nation, worship took on the cultural form and language of the people.

In 1542 Pope Paul III convened a council in the town of Trent. The Council of Trent, which lasted from 1545 to 1562 was interrupted several times by war. Trent was the start of the Counter-Reformation, which shaped Catholicism for almost four centuries, until Vatican II in the 1960s.

Among other things, the Council of Trent maintained:

• Christ remains in the consecrated host, even after the mass is over.
• Adoration of Christ in the Eucharist is legitimate, therefore, so are processions of the Blessed Sacrament.
• Communion under both species is not necessary to receive Christ whole and entire.
• The Mass is truly the sacrifice of Christ.
• The Mass may be offered for the living and for the dead.
• Christ ordains priests to offer his body and blood.

Because Trent had gone on for so long, the council did nothing about liturgical renewal. They decided to leave that to the pope. On July 14, 1570, Pope Pius V officially introduced a new missal. The missal was obligatory for the entire church, and it was unalterable. Nothing could be added, deleted, or changed. No language other than Latin could be used. Celebrants were ordered to use this missal as soon as possible. The papacy threatened sanctions against anyone who did not use the missal in the correct way. Pope Pius V also imposed a lectionary of biblical readings.

Scholars believe that the reason Pius V was so adamant that the missal be obligatory was that he was afraid the liturgy would become so diversified that the church would reach the point of anarchy. He also kept a tight rein on the printing of the missal to ensure it was error-free. Careful control of the printing process played an essential role in the success of this unifying project of the church.

The Missal of St. Pius V received a better reception than expected. Scholars have speculated that there was a need to "circle the wagons" or to close ranks around the pope in response to the Protestant revolt. After the reform of Pius V came Pope Sixtus V who reigned from 1585 to 1590. On January 22, 1588, Sixtus V created a department in the Curia called "the Congregation of Rites and Ceremonies." The responsibility of this congregation was to ensure that all sacred rites were strictly followed and observed by all people, in all places, and in all churches throughout the world.

Before this congregation was founded, individual churches had a certain amount of liberty and say in matters of liturgical ceremonies. Bishops and local councils lost virtually all control. The experts on rubrics took over the Mass. They anticipated possible deviations from the law. They cleared up doubts, argued fine points, and wrote volumes on the shape of the tabernacle, the length of the altar, how many times to genuflect, and how many candles to light for a High Mass.

The Liturgy and Vatican II

In January 1959, Pope John XXIII first mentioned his plan for the Second Vatican Council. If you examine the history of the half century leading up to Vatican II, you can see that liturgical reform had become inevitable. It was already in the making, but on a totally different track from the one taken by the Council of Trent. For example, in 1903, Pope Pius X insisted that Gregorian chant be sung by the people. In 1905, he called the faithful to frequent, even daily communion. In Belgium, new life was given to the liturgical movement in the monasteries and then brought to the people. Beginning in 1920, long-untranslated Mass prayers were made available to people in their own language, so they could follow along at Mass and achieve some degree of participation. In a monastery in Germany, a group of monks studied the ancient liturgy, paving a way for restoration.

In 1947, in his encyclical letter *Mediator Dei,* Pope Pius XII encouraged dialogue Masses. In the same encyclical, he defined the liturgy as "the worship rendered by the Mystical Body of Christ in the entirety of its Head and members" (20). This definition was later adopted by Vatican II. In other words, liturgy is not only worship by Jesus Christ or by the priest acting "in the person of Christ," it is worship by the entire church united to its head. The people must therefore act with the priest. In 1948, Pius XII established a commission for general liturgical reform.

At the opening session of the Second Vatican Council, the bishops immediately accepted the plan proposed for the *Constitution on the Sacred Liturgy* and began to work on it. After much discussion and revision, the document was voted on by the Fathers of the Council. The final vote was 2,146 in favor, 4 against. Pope Paul VI promulgated the plan on December 4, 1963.

As did *Mediator Dei,* the *Constitution on the Sacred Liturgy* emphasized the real presence of Jesus in the Eucharist. Vatican II saw liturgy as an action of Christ the priest and of his Body, the church. Liturgical celebration was seen as an action we do with Christ. The Second Vatican Council saw liturgy as "the summit toward which the activity of the Church is directed; at the same time it is the fount from which all [her] power flows" (10). In any statement Vatican II made about the word *church,* it was referring to all the faithful.

Another key word in the liturgy constitution is participation. Chapter One of the *Constitution on the Sacred Liturgy* calls for full participation in the Mass:

> The Church earnestly desires that all the faithful should be led to that full, conscious, and active participation in liturgical celebrations called for by the very nature of the liturgy. ... This full and active participation ... is the aim to be considered before all else. For it is the primary and indispensable source from which the faithful are to derive the true Christian spirit (14).

In Chapter Two, the liturgy constitution goes on to say:

> The Church, therefore, earnestly desires that Christ's faithful, when present at this mystery of faith, should not be there as strangers or silent spectators; on the contrary, through a good understanding of the rites and prayers they should take part in the sacred service conscious of what they are doing, with devotion and full involvement (48).

The liturgy constitution called for a new lectionary cycle of Scripture readings to be proclaimed at liturgy, the restoration of the homily, the prayers of the faithful, communion under both species, concelebration, and a revision of the liturgical year. It also opened the door to the use of the mother language of the people for Mass and it did not rule out the use of Latin in the liturgy. A new missal was promulgated by Pope Paul VI on April 3, 1969, and was revised with minor changes on Holy Thursday in 1975.

2

The Liturgy of the Word
And the Eucharist

The Mass is divided into two parts: the first part is called the Liturgy of the Word, and the second part is called the Liturgy of the Eucharist. The Liturgy of the Word has its roots in the Jewish temple word service, whereas, the Liturgy of the Eucharist traces itself back to the Last Supper. Within the Liturgy of the Word there are two parts: gather and proclaim. We also find two parts in the Liturgy of the Eucharist: break and send.

Gather

Church does not just happen. It is the role of the members of the assembly gathered for liturgy to make it happen. "Gathering" is an important action by which a roomful of individuals is transformed into an assembly. Gathering takes place only when people go out of their way to give attention to each other.

Gathering is difficult to do. It demands an amount of generosity. Gathering asks that all members of the assembly give of themselves to each other. Gathering is another name for "hospitality," the process we use to make people feel at home. It is the way we try to make strangers welcome. The rite of gathering is the way we make busy, preoccupied people glad they decided to come to our Catholic community.

Genuine gathering calls on us to break down the walls that keep us apart: walls of selfishness, walls of self-centeredness, and walls of simple shyness. Gathering is the first, indispensable step of Christian love. It is the first movement in fulfilling God's commandment to love one another.

The purpose of the gathering rite is to help the assembled people become a worshiping community by being ready to listen attentively to the Word of God, to receive Jesus in the Eucharist, and to be Christ to one another. The gathering rite takes place as soon as we get into our automobile to drive to liturgy and concludes with the opening prayer. The opening prayer or collect gathers all our prayers into one and leads us to the next step, the proclamation of the Word.

Proclaim

The task of the Catholic Church in our time is to give God's living Word back to the people. Vatican II insists that the Word of God is the first source of life.

" 'Gathering' is an important action by which a roomful
of individuals is transformed into an assembly."

The purpose of proclaiming the Word of God in the midst of the assembly gathered for liturgy is to help the assembly experience the life-giving presence of Jesus in his word. This experience of Jesus in the Word takes place only to the extent that members of the assembly consciously and deliberately take on the role of listeners. Proclamation in the midst of the assembly is the first purpose of all Scripture. From the beginning, God's Word has found its most important role in being proclaimed in the assemblies of God's people. We see this in the parables proclaimed by Jesus.

Lectors are encouraged not just to read the Word of God but to proclaim it. Members of the assembly should not be hearing the Word of God proclaimed at liturgy for the first time. They are encouraged to make the Scripture readings a part of their prayer life during the week by reading, studying, and reflecting.

At Sunday liturgy three readings are proclaimed and a (responsorial) psalm is sung. The first reading is from the Old Testament, which comes to the liturgy from the Jewish synagogue service. The first reading is usually connected to the Gospel reading by a similar theme.

The psalm or responsorial psalm also continues the practice of the Jewish synagogue. Christians have traditionally responded to a Scripture reading by singing a psalm. Today the community gathered for liturgy responds to the Word of God (the first reading) with the Word of God (responsorial psalm). The psalms were written to be sung; the responsorial psalm should never be spoken at Mass.

The second reading is always a New Testament reading, usually from Paul or another epistle. The choice of the Scripture text for Mass is made independently of the first reading and Gospel reading. In the second reading the assembly encounters the early church living the Christian faith. It provides the assembly an example of how to live and follow Jesus.

Since the earliest times the Gospel reading has been emphasized by special signs of respect: the priest or deacon proclaims it and the assembly stands to hear the reading. Standing is also seen as alertness in the presence of the risen Lord. The Gospel reading is the high point in the Liturgy of the Word; it proclaims the Good News of salvation by the risen Christ. It is Jesus Christ living and present among his people calling them to faith and conversion.

The Catholic Church divides its book of Scripture readings for liturgy, called the lectionary, into a three-year cycle: Cycle A, B and C. In Cycle A, the Gospel of Matthew is proclaimed for that liturgical year. Cycle B proclaims Mark, and Cycle C contains the Gospel of Luke. John's Gospel is proclaimed during the Sundays of Lent, the Easter Season, and certain Sundays during cycle B. The church's liturgical year begins on the First Sunday of Advent and ends with the feast of Christ the King.

After the Gospel reading, the homily takes place. The homily is meant to apply the scripture readings to the lives of the assembly, calling them to conversion and faithfulness to Jesus. The proclamation rite also includes the creed and the prayers of the faithful.

Break

The eucharistic prayer is the prayer of the church. It belongs to the whole church. St. Augustine said, "The church makes the Eucharist; the Eucharist makes the church." The entire assembly is the celebrant of the liturgy. It is the task of the entire assembly, led by the presider, to be fully active in making their contribution to the liturgy.

The eucharistic prayer is styled after the Jewish table-blessing prayer, which is a story of all that God has done for the Jewish people: calling them forth from slavery, bringing them into a new land, making them his chosen people, and sealing his promise with a faithful covenant. As the story unfolds, the people respond with their psalm songs of praise, blessing, and thanksgiving. The church's eucharistic prayer is also a story. By means of the eucharistic prayer, the church tells the same story of all that God has done, with special emphasis on the unique saving death and resurrection of Jesus.

The presider is the one who tells the story and calls the members of the assembly into the story. This storytelling is not just a memorial of the past actions of God and Jesus. It is a story of God's present action in the lives of all people in the world, particularly in the lives of those who are assembled at Mass.

The assembly prays the eucharistic prayer over bread and wine with the belief that through this prayer the elements of bread and wine are transformed into the Body and Blood of Jesus Christ. Jesus is truly present in the bread and wine following the words of consecration.

The Catholic Church offers the eucharistic prayer in the power of the Holy Spirit because it is only in the power of the Spirit that the transformation of bread and wine and of people's hearts can take place. Everything that God has done for his people has been done in the power of the Holy Spirit.

By and large, Catholics are very much aware of the transformation that the Spirit brings about in the bread and wine. It becomes the Body and Blood of Christ. However, Catholics are not very aware of the transformation that the Spirit wants to make of the people into the Body of Christ. This transformation is the reason for celebrating Sunday liturgy. Aquinas tells us that the peace and unity in the Body of Christ are the immediate effects of the Eucharist. As members of the assembly we are called to celebrate in such a way that other members of the assembly at Mass are helped to open themselves to a deeper relationship with Jesus through the power of the Holy Spirit.

Send

In most Catholic parishes, there is little ritual action at the dismissal. What actually happens is Sunday Mass sort of splits at the seams and spills out all over the place. People only seem to hear the "GO" part of the dismissal and they "GO" with gusto.

A substantial number begin their exodus immediately after communion. People begin to melt away. People depart just as they would from a ball game where the final outcome is very clear some minutes before the end. This creates an annoying division between those who stay for the entire Mass and those who leave early.

Why do some people leave Mass early? One reason to consider is that for centuries Catholics learned that Mass was an obligation under pain of mortal sin. Catholics learned that you fulfilled your obligation if you were physically present for the offertory, consecration, and communion.

The dismissal rite sends each member of the community forth to do good works, praising and blessing the Lord. Vatican II informs us that the eucharistic response of the assembly does not stop when Mass is over. The ultimate, and most important, eucharistic response is what you do after you go home. This is called mission and evangelization. As the assembly we are sent out as the Lord's disciples, not just as individuals but as "church" to proclaim the Good News of Jesus' love for all. We are sent forth to help, assist, and support one another to build up the Body of Christ.

As we "go in peace to love and serve the Lord" as Catholics, we are called to move beyond seeing Sunday liturgy as an obligation and leaving after communion. The Mass is about our relationship with Jesus and with others. Catholics are invited to be aware of their baptismal call and promise and to recognize that each person has a role in evangelization and a responsibility to assist others to "taste and see" the goodness of the Lord.

3

The Role of the Assembly At Liturgy

We are Christians because through the Christian community we have met Jesus Christ, heard his word in invitation, and responded to him in faith. We gather at Mass that we may hear and express our faith again in this assembly and, by expressing it, renew and deepen it.

... We come together to deepen our awareness of, and commitment to, the action of his Spirit in the whole of our lives at every moment. We come together to acknowledge the love of God poured out among us in the work of the Spirit, to stand in awe and praise.

We are celebrating when we involve ourselves meaningfully in the thoughts, words, songs, and gestures of the worshiping community—when everything we do is wholehearted and authentic for us—when we mean the words and want to do what is done.

People in love make signs of love, not only to express their love but also to deepen it. Love never expressed dies. Christians' love for Christ and for one another and Christians' faith in Christ and in one another must be expressed in the signs and symbols of celebration or they will die (*Music in Catholic Worship* 1–4).

The word *liturgy* comes from the Greek word *leitourgia*. It literally means "the people's work." It is a public work done for the service of others. In ancient Greek it originally meant civic duty or the cooperation of all citizens to make society work.

The religious meaning of liturgy is similar. Liturgy is defined as public worship for the service of others. Liturgy is public prayer and ritual; it is communal in nature. There is nothing private about the liturgy.

As Christians we are called to be Christ to others. By our baptism we have a responsibility to allow the light of Jesus to shine in our lives and in the lives of others. We are called by Christ to be of service, and this attitude is required of us at liturgy. In a sense all of us are required to work at liturgy. So many times you will hear people being critical of the priest or the music at Mass, but what about the people who are passive at liturgy, those who do not sing, participate, reach out to others, or who leave early?

Some people say, "I don't get anything out of it." It is important to note that this attitude is never taught in Scripture. Where in Scripture does Jesus teach that you should not do something unless you benefit from it? This attitude is also not present in the sacred tradition of the church. Where in tradition is it taught that Jesus did not do something unless he got something out of it?

The specific purpose of the Mass is to serve the community. We come to Mass to be of service, to give praise and worship to God, and to bring others to Christ. We do not come to Mass for ourselves.

"Our responsibility is to support one another in public worship."

Just as in daily living, you have up and down days; so too is that fluctuation present in gathering on Sunday. Our responsibility is to support one another in public worship. On the up days you give; on the down days you receive. As Catholics we do not come to Mass for ourselves, but for others, so that others can experience Jesus through the Word, the Eucharist, and us.

Here is what the *General Instruction of the Roman Missal* says on this topic:

> In the celebration of Mass the faithful are a holy people, a people God has made his own, a royal priesthood: they give thanks to the Father and offer [Jesus] not only through the hands of the priest but also together with him and learn to offer themselves. ...
>
> They therefore are to shun any appearance of individualism or division, keeping before their mind that they have the one Father in heaven and therefore are all brothers and sisters to each other. They should become one body, whether by hearing the word of God, or joining in prayers and song, or above all by offering the sacrifice together and sharing together in the Lord's table. There is a beautiful expression of this unity when their faithful maintain uniformity in their actions and in standing, sitting, or kneeling (62).

In their document *Environment and Art in Catholic Worship*, the Catholic bishops note:

> Among the symbols with which liturgy deals, none is more important than this assembly of believers. ...
>
> The most powerful experience of the sacred is found in the celebration and the persons celebrating, that is, it is found in the action of the assembly: the living words, the living gestures, the living sacrifice, the living meal. This was at the heart of the earliest liturgies. Evidence of this is found in their architectural floor plans which were designed as general gathering spaces,

spaces which allowed the whole assembly to be part of the action.

… The entire congregation is an active component. There is no audience, no passive element in the liturgical celebration (28–30).

The goal of the liturgy is the transformation of people's lives to Jesus; it is about the conversion of hearts. The Catholic bishops teach us that good liturgy builds faith, while poor liturgy destroys it (*Music in Catholic Worship* 6). The Catholic Church asks that we make our liturgies life-giving, and each of us plays a vital role in that request through full, active, and conscious participation in the liturgy. We can accomplish this by: (1) making sure we come early or on time for Mass, (2) having a spirit of Christian hospitality by reaching out to others, (3) actively praying and singing during the liturgy, and (4) staying for the entire Mass.

God has gifted all with an ability to dream. Envision for a moment a Catholic community that is alive (see Chapter 6), where people want to be at Mass and to share the Christ within them, where there is a spirit of Christian hospitality and love, where people are actively praying and singing all the songs, and where everyone stays for the entire Mass! It can be done, and it starts with you as a member of the assembly.

4

Music at Liturgy

Let the word of Christ, rich as it is, dwell in you. In wisdom made perfect, instruct and admonish one another. Sing gratefully to God from your hearts in psalms, hymns, and inspired songs (Col 3:16).

The *Constitution of the Sacred Liturgy* desires that all the faithful should be led to full, conscious, and active participation in liturgical celebrations (14). Yet observing the assembly during liturgy reveals that many Catholics do not sing and participate in the Mass. According to Cardinal Roger Mahony in *Gather Faithfully Together,* "Full participation brings us to the liturgy, body and soul, with all our might. ... Full participation also means that a baptized person does not mentally weave in and out of the liturgy. Our duty is not just to be present; our duty is to be fully present. The songs are for singing" (91, 92).

In *Guide for the Assembly,* Cardinal Joseph Bernadin writes about the importance of music in liturgy:

> Liturgy is our song. We sing the liturgy. Song is not a frill but is part of the central action itself. What we do in the liturgy is too vast and too deep to be left to our speaking voices. We need music so that we can fully express what we are about (31).

The *General Instruction of the Roman Missal* (GIRM) states that great importance should be attached to the use of singing at Mass (19). The *Constitution on the Sacred Liturgy* says that "a liturgical service takes on a nobler aspect when the rites are celebrated with singing, the sacred ministers take their parts in them, and the faithful actively participate" (113). Joseph Gelineau in *Learning to Celebrate* says:

> Singing gives added flavor and meaning to the words that are said and heard. It lends to the spoken word its full strength of expression and communion. Singing unites those who sing. Use of the same tone and rhythm produces not only unison of harmony but a community. Singing is celebration. It takes us beyond ordinary duties and practical tasks, opening out onto other aspects of existence: gratuitousness, freedom, love (48).

Music in Catholic Worship, written by the Bishops' Committee on the Liturgy, says that music in liturgy serves the expression of faith:

> Among the many signs and symbols used by the Church to celebrate its faith, music is of preeminent importance. As sacred song united to words it forms a necessary or integral part of the solemn liturgy (Cf. CSL 112). Yet the function of music is ministerial; it must serve and never dominate. Music should assist the assembled believers to express and share the gift of faith that is within them and to nourish and strengthen their inte-

"Singing gives added flavor and meaning to the words that are said and heard. It lends to the spoken word its full strength of expression and communion. Singing unites those who sing."

rior commitment of faith. It should heighten the texts so that they speak more fully and more effectively. The quality of joy and enthusiasm which music adds to community worship cannot be gained in any other way. It imparts a sense of unity to the congregation and sets the appropriate tone for a particular celebration. In addition to expressing texts, music can also unveil a dimension of meaning and feeling, a communication of ideas and intuitions which words alone cannot yield. This dimension is integral to the human personality and to growth in faith (23, 24).

In choosing music for liturgy, musicians are asked by the church to seek out and create quality worship music. The music should be technically, aesthetically, and expressively pleasing. "To determine the value of a given musical element in a liturgical celebration a threefold judgment must be made: musical, liturgical, and pastoral" (*Music in Catholic Worship* 25). "Music for the congregation must be within its members' performance capability. The congregation must be comfortable and secure with what they are doing in order to celebrate well" (*Music in Catholic Worship* 34).

Within the liturgy there are many different elements that may be sung at liturgy according to *Music in Catholic Worship*. They include acclamations, processionals, responsorial psalms, ordinary chants, supplementary songs, and litanies.

"The acclamations are shouts of joy which arise from the whole assembly as forceful and meaningful assents to God's Word and Action. They are important because they make some of the most significant moments of the Mass (Gospel, eucharistic prayer, Lord's Prayer) stand out" (*Music in Catholic Worship* 53). In liturgy, five acclamations should be sung at Mass: the Alleluia; the Holy, Holy; the Memorial Acclamation; the Great Amen; and the Doxology to the Lord's Prayer.

Music in Catholic Worship notes the gathering song and the communion song are processional chants. They are vital "for creating and sustaining an awareness of community" (60).

The entrance song should create an atmosphere of celebration. It helps put the assembly in proper frame of mind for listening to the Word of God. It helps people to become conscious of themselves as a worshiping community. The communion song should foster a sense of unity. It should be simple and not demand great effort (61, 62).

The responsorial psalm should always be sung since the psalms are songs. The responsorial psalm is a response to the first reading. "The liturgy of the Word comes more fully to life if between the first two readings a cantor sings the psalm and all sing the response" (*Music in Catholic Worship* 63).

The next category is ordinary chants, which includes the Kyrie (Lord, have mercy), the Gloria, the Lord's Prayer, the Lamb of God or Agnus Dei, and the Profession of Faith or creed. Traditionally the Gloria and the Lamb of God are sung. But according to *Music in Catholic Worship*, ordinary chants may be sung or said, and which is sung or said may depend on different circumstances (64).

Supplementary songs include the offertory song, which accompanies the procession and preparation of the gifts, the psalm or song after communion, and the recessional song. This category is considered to include the least important songs in the liturgy because there are no requirements by the church that these songs be said or sung. With these songs, the choir may have a more pronounced role.

The final category is litanies. *Music in Catholic Worship* states:

Litanies are often more effective when sung. The repetition of melody and rhythm draws the people together in a strong and unified response. In addition to the "Lamb of God," ... the general intercessions (prayer of the faithful) offer an opportunity for litanical singing, as do the invocations of Christ in the penitential rite (74).

The *Constitution of the Sacred Liturgy* notes the importance of music in liturgy and of the assembly's full participation in the liturgy. "The musical tradition of the universal Church is a treasure of inestimable value, greater even than that of any other art." The main reason for this pre-eminence is that, as sacred song closely bound to the text, it forms a necessary or integral part of the solemn liturgy. Liturgical worship is given a more noble form when the divine offices are celebrated solemnly in song with the assistance of sacred ministers and the active participation of the people (112, 113).

5

Environment and Space
In Liturgy

The history of liturgy in the Catholic Church has shown that liturgy has taken place in a wide variety of places and settings: for example, a post–Vatican II church structure, a home, on a ship, in a field in the midst of war, in a hospital chapel, on a beach, in a forest, or in a cathedral.

We Gather in Christ, Our Identity as Assembly, from the Archdiocese of Cincinnati, states:

In the minds of many modern Christians, the Gothic cathedral represents the ideal architectural form for worship. However, the ecclesiology it expresses and the liturgy it makes possible differ greatly from the church's present understanding of itself and liturgical theology. A study of the plan shows a long, narrow nave (where the people stood), a choir area (where the monks sang the daily office), and at a considerable distance from the people, the sanctuary with the altar. Clearly, this worship space reflects a view of the church that centers on the monastic community and encourages passivity on the part of the laity. The placement of the altar at such a distance from the worshiping assembly made it difficult to see what was happening and also made a profound statement about the ordinary person's worthiness to approach the sacred too closely. Indeed, the members of the worshiping assembly received the Eucharist infrequently. At that point in church history, the liturgy was the concern of the official church—the clergy. For centuries to come, the design and construction of many magnificent ecclesiastical edifices would be impacted by this understanding of the assembly's role as spectators and not active participants in the liturgy (41).

The importance of the liturgical environment is vital to good liturgy. Where we sing and participate from in the liturgy greatly enhances or distracts from the celebration.

When a parish begins the process of building a new church or renovating an existing one, many questions and concerns arise. The *Constitution on the Sacred Liturgy* says when churches are built, great care must be taken so that they are suitable for the celebration of liturgical services and for the active participation of the faithful (124).

Environment and Art in Catholic Worship also notes that "benches or chairs for seating of the assembly should be so constructed and arranged that they maximize feelings of community and involvement (*General Instruction of the Roman Missal* 273). The arrangement should facilitate a clear view not only of the one who presides and the multiple focal points of reading, preaching, praying, music and movement during the rite, but also of other members of the congregation" (68).

Built of Living Stones: Art, Architecture, and Worship expands on that idea, stating:

> Styles of benches, pews, or chairs can be found that comfortably accommodate the human form. Kneelers or kneeling cushions should also be provided so that the whole congregation can easily kneel when the liturgy calls for it. Parishes will want to choose a seating arrangement that calls the congregation to active participation and that avoids any semblance of a theater or an arena. It is also important that the seating plan provide spaces for an unimpeded view of the sanctuary by people in wheelchairs or with walkers. Experience indicates that space in the front or at the sides of the church is better than in the rear where a standing congregation obscures the view of those seated in wheelchairs at the back of the church (19).

The primary symbols of the liturgy, the assembly, the altar, the ambo, and the presider's chair should be positioned in a way so they are prominent. Liturgical designers say that no one should be more than sixty feet away from the sanctuary area.

How the community gathers for liturgy is important. The narthex or vestibule of the church or the area just outside the church building serves as the gathering space. Liturgical designers state the gathering space should convey an atmosphere of welcome and hospitality where people can greet and converse. This area should help the people gathering for liturgy know they are entering a sacred space. Added items such as posters, signs, cluttered tables, bulletin boards, and boxes communicate an attitude of indifference, confusion, and chaos.

The Baptismal Font

In the early church, buildings called baptistries were constructed for baptism. The font was big enough for an adult to be immersed in. The word *baptize* means "to dip"; the word *immersion* means that the person stands or kneels in inches of water, while large amounts of water are poured over him or her. Scholars speculate that these baptismal fonts were not big enough for adults to be submerged in. Submersion means that the entire body goes underwater. As infant baptism became more the custom and norm, the baptismal font was moved into the church and became smaller. With the revision of the rites of baptism (1969, 1972, and 1988) and the restoration of the Easter Vigil (1951), the baptismal font is regaining its important place.

The baptismal font should be located at the entrance of the church. Each time the assembly gathers for liturgy, they can touch the waters and mark themselves with the sign of the cross as a reminder of their own baptism.

> Because the rites of initiation of the Church begin with baptism and are completed by the reception of the Eucharist, the baptismal font and its location reflect the Christian's journey through the waters of baptism to the altar. This integral relationship between the baptismal font and the altar can be demonstrated in a variety of ways, such as placing the font and altar on the same architectural axis, using natural or artificial lighting, using the same floor patterns, and using common or similar materials and elements of design.

> … For this reason the font should be visible and accessible to all who enter the church building. While the baptistry is proportioned to the building itself and should be able to hold a good number of people, its actual size will be determined by the needs of the local community (*Built of Living Stones* 16).

Baptismal fonts should be constructed so that adult catechumens and infants may be immersed. According to *Environment and Art in Catholic Worship*, "immersion is the fuller and more appropriate symbolic action in baptism (*Rite of Baptism for Children* (BC), introduction)" (76). It is in the living waters of baptism that people are reborn in Jesus Christ.

The Ambo

The ambo is the table of the Word, which is used for the proclamation of the Word of God and the homily. It has also been called a pulpit or lectern. According to *Environment and Art in Catholic Worship*, the ambo represents "the dignity and uniqueness of the Word of God and of reflection upon that Word" (74). *Built of Living Stones* states of the ambo:

> Here the Christian community encounters the living Lord in the word of God and prepares itself for the "breaking of the bread" and the mission to live the word that will be proclaimed. An ample area around the ambo is needed to allow a Gospel procession with a full complement of ministers bearing candles and incense (15).

The word *ambo* has its origin in the Greek verb *anabainein,* which means "to go up." During the Middle Ages a large, elevated platform was called an ambo. The Scriptures were proclaimed from this raised surface.

For hundreds of years the ambo played an obscure role in the liturgy. The focal point of the pre–Vatican II Mass was the altar. The altar had an "epistle side" and a "Gospel side." The Scriptures were not proclaimed from one space, but divided into two places.

The ambo is used for the proclamation of the Scriptures, the responsorial psalm, the homily, and the prayers of the faithful (also called the general intercessions). The ambo is not the place for announcements, talks, or to lead the singing (unless it is the responsorial psalm). It is reserved for God's word only.

Additionally, the ambo "should be beautifully designed, constructed of fine materials, and proportioned carefully and simply for its function" (*Environment and Art in Catholic Worship* 74). The *General Instruction of the Roman Missal* says:

> The dignity of the word of God requires the church to have a place that is suitable for proclamation of the word and is a natural focal point for the people during the liturgy of the word (*Inter Oecumenici* 96). As a rule the lectern or ambo should be stationary, not simply a movable stand. In keeping with the structure of each church, it must be so placed that the ministers may be easily seen and heard by the faithful (272).

The ambo is the place where the Word of God is proclaimed to the community and reflected upon.

The Presider's Chair

The presider's or presidential chair has it origins in the Latin word *cathedra*. The cathedra was the chair of a high-ranking civic official. The church took the concept of the chair and incorporated it into the liturgy. From his chair the bishop presided over the liturgy. The word *cathedral* comes from the word *cathedra*, which means the house of the bishop's chair.

As church architecture developed, the bishop's chair was placed on a podium. It was like a king's throne. In the fourth century, as parishes began to be created and developed, the presider's chair became much simpler in design and less ornate and florid. Later the presider's chair almost became obsolete since the priest stood at the altar for most of the Mass. Within Vatican II's liturgical reforms, the church worked to recapture the significance of the presider's chair.

According to *Built of Living Stones*, "an appropriate placement of the chair allows the priest celebrant to be visible to all in the congregation. The chair reflects the dignity of the one who leads the community in the person of Christ, but is never intended to be remote or grandiose. The priest celebrant's chair is distinguished

"The ambo is the table of the Word, which is used for the proclamation of the Word of God and the homily.... (It) represents 'the dignity and uniqueness of the Word of God and of reflection upon that Word.'"

from the seating for other ministers by its design and placement"
(15).

It is from the chair that the presider calls the assembly to prayer,
listens to the Word of God, preaches, professes the faith of the
church, invites prayers and petitions, announces community
activities, and blesses the people as they are sent forth from the
liturgy.

The Altar

The history of the altar is a rich one. Through the centuries the
shape, design, and placement of the altar has changed.

The word *altar* has its origins in two languages. Altar comes
from the Latin *altare,* which comes from another Latin word
adolere, which means "to burn." The Greeks used the word
thysiasterion which denotes the table of sacrifice. It was at a table that
Jesus presided at the Last Supper and gave us the gift of the
Eucharist. The church continues this tradition at the altar. At the
altar the church celebrates the paschal mystery: the life, death, and
resurrection of Christ.

During the first centuries, the early Christian community
gathered around a free-standing table for the breaking of the bread.
As centuries passed and the church's understanding of liturgy
changed, so did the design and location of the altar. No longer was
the altar a free-standing table; it grew in length and in artistic
expression. As the Mass became more intricate and detailed, the
altar was placed at the rear of the sanctuary area. The priest would
celebrate Mass with his back to the people. The altar also became
longer because the two Scripture readings were read at each side of
the altar. The eucharistic prayer, which included the consecration,
took place in the middle of the altar. Eventually the tabernacle was
placed on the altar.

With the Second Vatican Council the Catholic Church returned
to its roots concerning the altar. The altar was moved from the back

wall of the apse and positioned so the presider would face the assembly. In a sense, it became a free-standing table again. The altar did not need to be elongated because the Scripture readings for liturgy were to be proclaimed at the ambo. The tabernacle was moved off the altar, preferably to a chapel of reservation. This was done because communion should be shared from the liturgy that the assembly was participating in, and not from a previous Mass. The tabernacle's primary function is reservation of communion for the sick; the secondary function is adoration. The tabernacle is not meant to supply Eucharist for liturgy.

Environment and Art in Catholic Worship states:

> The altar, the holy table, should be the most noble, the most beautifully designed and constructed table the community can provide (GI nos. 259–270; Appendix to GI no. 263). It is the common table of the assembly, a symbol of the Lord, at which the presiding minister stands and upon which are placed the bread and wine and their vessels and the book. It is holy and sacred to this assembly's action and sharing, so it is never used as a table of convenience or as a resting place for papers, notes, cruets, or anything else. It stands free, approachable from every side, capable of being encircled. It is desirable that candles, cross, any flowers or other decoration in the area should not be so close to the altar as to constitute impediments to anyone's approach or movement around the common table (71).

In terms of design, *Built on Living Stones* states:

> Although there is no specified size or shape for an altar, it should be in proportion to the church. The shape and size should reflect the nature of the altar as the place of sacrifice and the table around which Christ gathers the community to nourish them. In considering the dimensions of the altar, parishes will also want to insure that the other major furnishings in the sanctuary are in harmony and proportion to the altar.

The mensa should be large enough to accommodate the priest celebrant, the deacon, and the acolytes who minister there and should be able to hold *The Sacramentary* [*The Roman Missal*] and the vessels with the bread and wine. Impact and focal quality are not only related to placement, size, or shape, but also especially to the quality of the altar's design and worthiness of its construction. The altar should be centrally located in the sanctuary and the center of attention in the church.

During the Liturgy of the Eucharist, the altar must be visible from all parts of the church but not so elevated that it causes visual or symbolic division from the liturgical assembly. Methods of elevation can be found that still allow access to the altar by ministers who need wheelchairs or who have other disabilities (14–15).

The altar is a holy and sacred place in the church building; that is why the presider kisses the altar at the beginning and ending of each liturgy. It is at the holy table, the altar, that the assembly is nourished and strengthened with the Bread of Life.

The Tabernacle

The tabernacle contains the bread that has been consecrated at liturgy. The word tabernacle comes from the Latin *tabernaculum* which means "tent." The tabernacle traces its roots to the Jewish meeting tent, which is where the Ark of the Covenant dwelled. In Jewish thinking this embodied the presence of God among the people.

Tabernacles started in the second century when a small amount of the consecrated bread was placed in a pyx and taken to a member of the community who was ill and could not attend liturgy. At first this was the only reason for the reservation of the Blessed Sacrament because everything (the Body and Blood of Christ) was consumed, except for what was reserved for the sick.

In the Middle Ages, devotion to the Blessed Sacrament grew mainly because people were sharing in communion less and less. People at this time were adoring the Blessed Sacrament rather than sharing in communion. The primary purpose of the Eucharist is to be consumed and for people to be nourished by the Bread of Life. The custom of a permanent container for reservation of the Blessed Sacrament on the main altar was in place by the sixteenth century.

In addition to reserving communion for the sick and serving for adoration of the Blessed Sacrament, the tabernacle also held extra hosts for Mass. At communion the priest could always go to the tabernacle for extra hosts if necessary. The tabernacle was being used to store hosts for Mass.

As mentioned earlier, the primary function of the tabernacle is the reservation of the communion for the sick. Adoration of the Blessed Sacrament is important in the life of a Catholic, but it is apart from the liturgy. The church has stated that the assembly should be fed the bread and wine consecrated at the liturgy they are attending not from an earlier liturgy. The *General Instruction of the Roman Missal* states, "It is most desirable that the faithful should receive the Lord's body from hosts consecrated at the same mass and that, in the instances when it is permitted, they share in the chalice" (56h). The tabernacle serves the sick, while the altar serves the people at liturgy.

The location of the tabernacle has given rise to debates in the church. At times the discussions have become intense because Catholics have strong feelings about the Eucharist.

The document *Holy Communion and the Worship of the Eucharist Outside of Mass* says the reservation and adoration of the Eucharist "will be achieved more easily if the (tabernacle) chapel is separate from the body of the church" (9).

Environment and Art in Catholic Worship states:

> The *celebration* of the eucharist is the focus of the normal Sunday assembly. As such, the major space of a church is designed for this *action*. Beyond the celebration of the eucha-

rist, the Church has had a most ancient tradition of reserving the eucharistic bread. The purpose of this reservation is to bring communion to the sick and to be the object of private devotion. Most appropriately, this reservation should be designated in a space designed for individual devotion. A room or chapel specifically designed and separate from the major space is important so that no confusion can take place between the celebration of the eucharist and reservation (GI no. 276). Active and static aspects of the same reality cannot claim the same human attention at the same time. Having the eucharist reserved in a place apart does not mean it has been relegated to a secondary place of no importance. Rather, a space carefully designed and appointed can give proper attention to the reserved sacrament (78).

However, according to *Built of Living Stones,* which was approved by the U.S. bishops on November 16, 2000:

There has been a shift in directives about the placement of the tabernacle over time. The latest edition of the *General Instruction of the Roman Missal* (2000) alters the earlier directive in GIRM, no. 276, which gave a clear preference for reservation in a separate chapel. GIRM, no. 315, now directs the diocesan bishop to determine the appropriate placement either in the sanctuary (including on the old altar which is no longer used for celebration) or in a separate chapel. It may not be reserved on the altar at which the Eucharist is celebrated (footnote 99).

The church has specific criteria for the tabernacle:

The tabernacle, as a receptacle for the reservation of the eucharist, should be solid and unbreakable, dignified and properly ornamented (GI no. 277). It may be placed in a wall niche, on a pillar, eucharistic tower. It should not be placed on an altar for the altar is a place for action not for reservation. There should be only one tabernacle in a church building. A lamp should burn continuously near it (*Environment and Art in Catholic Worship* 80).

Prayer, reflection, and adoration occurs best in a private, contemplative, and quiet space. Churches are full of activity: choir and music rehearsals, the decorating by the art and environment committee, cleaning, wedding rehearsals, and the liturgy. These types of activities do not allow a place for adoration and reflective prayer. A eucharistic chapel separate from the church meets the community's needs for quiet and individual prayer and devotion to the Blessed Sacrament. The eucharistic chapel should accommodate different prayer postures, including sitting, standing, kneeling, and prostrating.

More and more parishes today, through renovation or new construction projects in accord with the ancient tradition of the Catholic Church, are providing places of honor for the tabernacle as a sign of reverence, respect, and love for the Eucharist. This is the practice at St. Peter's Basilica in Rome. The tabernacle is not in the main sanctuary, but in a eucharistic chapel created for reservation for the sick and adoration and devotion to the Blessed Sacrament.

The Ambry

During Holy Week the bishop of each diocese presides over the Chrism Mass. At this liturgy the three oils that will be used for anointing the catechumens and for the sacraments of baptism, confirmation, holy orders, and the anointing of the sick are blessed. After the liturgy, the oils are brought to each parish. The oils for anointing catechumen and anointing the sick are simply blessed olive oil. Chrism, which is used for baptism, confirmation, and holy orders, is a mixture of olive oil and balsam. Chrism is also used in the consecration of churches and altars.

The ambry is where the containers of oil are stored. The word *ambry* comes from the Latin *armarium* which means "cupboard, chest, or safe." At times the holy oils were stored along with the Eucharist. As the tabernacle grew in importance for the reservation of the Blessed Sacrament, the holy oils were placed in the sacristy, or in a cupboard called an ambry.

The ambry and the display of the oils reminds the community of the sacramental importance of welcoming new members, confirming others in the faith, and caring for the ill.

The containers or vessels that hold the chrism should be large to indicate the importance of the oil and the sacraments they represent. The containers may be made of glass, wood, or metal. Each vessel has initials on it. The initials SC (*sacrum chrisma*) indicate the oil used in the sacraments of confirmation and holy orders. The sacrament of baptism uses OC (*oleum catechumenorum*), and OI (*oleum infirmorum*) is dispensed in the anointing of the sick.

The Reconciliation Chapel

Prior to Vatican II, the sacrament of reconciliation took place in a confessional. The confessional was small and dark. It contained a kneeler, as well as a screen or grill that separated the priest and the penitent. The penitent would walk into the confessional, close the door, kneel. In near darkness, he or she would wait for the priest to slide the screen open. Then the penitent would confess his or her sins, receive penance, and then receive absolution. Sometimes it was a daunting and overwhelming experience, especially for children.

Since Vatican II, the church has tried to focus on the unconditional forgiveness of God through the sacrament of reconciliation. The spiritual effects of the sacrament are reconciliation with God and the church community, as well as increased spiritual strength for the Christian journey.

The bishops of the United States have said that churches should have a separate chapel for the sacrament of reconciliation. In the

December 1974 issue of the *Bishops' Committee on Liturgy Newsletter*, they state:

> Small chapels or rooms of reconciliation should be provided in which penitents might choose to confess their sins and seek sacramental reconciliation through an informal face to face exchange with the priest.

In his article "The Reconciliation Chapel," Phillip Horrigan states:

> In keeping with our understanding of the sacrament of reconciliation as an experience of conversion and reclaiming our baptismal identity, the chapel of reconciliation could be located in relationship to the baptismal font. Since reconciliation returns us to the common table, the eucharistic gathering, it is appropriate for the reconciliation chapel to open into the main worship area.

Environment and Art in Catholic Worship notes:

> A room or rooms for the reconciliation of individual penitents may be located near the baptismal area (when that is at the entrance) or in another convenient place (Rite of Penance, nos. 12, 18b; *Bishop's Committee on the Liturgy Newsletter* 1965–1975, p. 450). Furnishings and decoration should be simple and austere, offering the penitent a choice between face-to-face encounter or the anonymity provided by a screen, with nothing superfluous in evidence beyond a simple cross, table and bible. The purpose of this room is primarily for the celebration of the reconciliation liturgy (81).

Due to the seriousness and importance of the sacrament of reconciliation, the Catholic community deserves a space that speaks of confession, contrition, penance, and reconciliation. The chapel should be a permanent fixture in the church, not something that is set up in an office or classroom. It should be a holy and sacred space for prayer that fosters forgiveness, peace, and reconciliation.

Statues, Shrines, and Stained Glass

Some Catholics are concerned about the lack of statues, images of saints, and stained glass in post–Vatican II church architecture.

Statues of saints and stained glass became prominent in church architecture when the language of the liturgy was not of the people's (in the vernacular) but in Latin. Because people had a difficult time understanding and hearing what was going on during Mass, the faithful began personal prayers and devotions to the saints and the Blessed Virgin Mary. This was done during Mass because the liturgy was not meeting the spiritual needs of the people. The statues and the depictions of the saints were a reminder to the faithful of the Christians who persevered in their faith and followed Christ. In addition to depicting the lives of the saints, stained glass was used to illustrate biblical scenes. Statues and stained glass were meant to deepen the faith of people.

Because the saints and devotions have an important role in the life of a Catholic, they deserve a prominent place in the life of the Catholic community. The *General Instruction of the Roman Missal* (GIRM) encourages devotions to the saints but in proper context in relation to the liturgy. In the church what should be central is the ambo, the altar, the presider's chair, and the assembly. According to the GIRM, statues should be limited and situated so they do not distract the people's attention from the celebration of the liturgy (278). In pre–Vatican II church architecture, statues, stained glass, and images of saints took up a large amount of space in the worship area.

Today in the narthex and the corners of the church, shrines that are significant or important to the community are being developed. These statues or images of saints can incorporate a healthy devotion and respect to the saints in proper relation to the liturgy. Some Catholic communities have commissioned stained glass depictions of biblical scenes that are significant to the community. Statues of saints that are important to the community could be placed in the gathering or welcoming space just outside the church building. This symbolizes the communion of saints encircling the Catholic Church of today as the people proceed into the church for liturgy.

6

A Prayerful Hope
And Vision For Liturgy

This narrative is a prayer and a vision of what liturgy could look like in the Catholic Church. Inspired by *Gather Faithfully Together* by Cardinal Roger Mahony of the Archdiocese of Los Angeles, this vision was written for St. Patrick Catholic Community in Scottsdale, Arizona, as part of the ongoing liturgical catechesis that takes place in the parish. The principles of liturgy that are dealt with in this account can be taken from St. Patrick's and applied to any liturgical community seeking to renew itself through liturgy. The church reminds us that because the liturgy is the work of the people, it is important that all see their role as vital during Mass. The purpose and intent of the liturgy is the transformation and conversion of people's hearts to Jesus Christ.

The People Gather

It is twenty minutes before the start of the 10:15 AM liturgy at St. Patrick's, and the music director and several members of the parish choir are going over some last-minute music fine-tuning. The ministers of hospitality, the servers, the readers, and the eucharistic ministers begin to arrive at the church and go about their duties. The communion ministers set up for Mass, making sure there is enough bread and wine, as well as communion bowls and chalices for the assembly to share in the Body and Blood of Christ. One eucharistic minister takes the bread and wine to the back of church for the procession of gifts. The ministers of hospitality pass out the songsheets to each person who enters the church and welcomes them to St. Patrick's in a spirit of Christian hospitality. The servers light the candles by the altar and ambo and check to make sure the sacramentary is in the right place. The readers go over their readings one last time and read over the prayers of the faithful. They are careful to ensure that they correctly pronounce the names of the sick and deceased. Some early comers are in the church, praying quietly or saying hello to fellow parishioners.

Throughout the neighborhood the gathering rite to the 10:15 AM Mass is taking place. Some families are running late, trying to get the children dressed and ready to go. A few are finishing breakfast, mindful of the one-hour fast before liturgy. Parishioners from the local nursing home board the bus that will take them to liturgy. In a small number of homes, they choose not to have the television or radio on or even read the Sunday paper. Instead they read and pray the Scripture readings that will be proclaimed at Mass. Not only has the presider prepared and prayed with the Scripture readings, the assembly has as well. Families, couples, and single people get into their automobiles and begin, from all directions, north and south, east and west, the procession to St. Patrick's for the 10:15 AM liturgy. All are welcomed at St. Patrick's.

In the sacristy, the presider is vested and prays in a hand-held circle with the communion ministers, servers, and readers. With just ten minutes before Mass, the choir sings a song that will be used in a future liturgy. The intent is to familiarize the people with new liturgical music. As the people enter the church, they pass by the baptismal font and take water from it, blessing themselves as a reminder of their own baptism. The ministers of hospitality continue to welcome parishioners, pass out songsheets, and help families and individuals find seats. They first try to fill the seats that are closest to the altar and ambo. They are also conscious of people who have young children or individuals who are in wheelchairs. The community of St. Patrick's has made it their practice to fill up the seats in the front of the church first. It is part of Christian hospitality for those who may come later to the liturgy. They also try to fill in each row from the center, so that people do not have to climb over each other. At 10:10 AM the music director invites the people to warm up their voices and practice singing the sending forth song. After the short practice, the presider comes forward and welcomes the members of the assembly gathered for liturgy. He asks anyone who is visiting to please stand and finds out where they are from. The assembly welcomes them with applause. So that no one is a stranger, the presider asks the people to welcome those individuals who are standing around them.

The music director announces the gathering song and everyone reaches for their songsheets, stands, and sings. The server leads the procession carrying the cross, the lector holds the lectionary, and the presider follows. All are singing. As the presider reaches the altar, he reverences it with a kiss, mindful of what takes place on this holy table. At the presider's chair, he continues to sing with the rest of the assembly. When the singing ends all the members of the assembly mark themselves with the sign of the cross: Father, Son, and Holy Spirit. The presider briefly introduces the liturgy. The penitential rite is said, but it may also be sung or chanted. The Gloria is always sung. At the end of the gathering rite all are invited, "Let us pray." The assembly responds with "Amen," a sign that they do believe. At this time the children are dismissed for their own Liturgy of the Word, which will take place at their level of understanding.

The Word Proclaimed

All are seated, waiting, almost anticipating the Word of God to be proclaimed. The minister of the Word is seated too. So that are all attentive, the lector will wait for fifteen to twenty seconds before proceeding to the ambo to proclaim the Scripture reading. There are no missalettes at St. Patrick's; there is no need for them. The people come prepared to hear the readings proclaimed. Each week in the bulletin there is an article titled "Pray the Sunday Readings," which gives a summary of the Scripture readings for the following Sunday. The people at St. Patrick's read the synopsis, open their Bibles during the week, prayerfully read the readings, and allow the passages for next Sunday's liturgy to become a part of their daily prayer life.

During the week the lector has prepared the reading as well. The lectors at St. Patrick's use a resource that is specifically designed for them. This book contains the Scripture readings, a summary of the readings, what should be emphasized in each reading, and a pronunciation guide. This publication comes in handy. Each minister of the Word has gone through a diocesan-mandated training process that has carefully prepared them for their ministry. The lector realizes it is an awesome responsibility to proclaim the Word of God to the people gathered for Sunday liturgy.

The lector opens the lectionary and proclaims; the people are listening. In today society's it is difficult to listen, but the people of St. Patrick's are attentive. They know how to listen; it has become an art. When the lector has completed the reading, the assembly responds, "Thanks be to God." There is silence again, before the responsorial psalm, before the second reading, and again before the Gospel is proclaimed. People use this silence to focus on what was just proclaimed.

"The Holy Spirit transforms bread and wine into the Body and Blood of Christ."

The homilist comes forward to break open the Word of God and apply it to people's lives. The homilist knows he has a difficult task and has prepared carefully for it. During the week he has prayed over the readings, reviewed material about the particular passages, met with the parish staff to discuss the readings, and set aside a considerable amount of time to prepare the homily. Because the people of St. Patrick's are good listeners they know right away if the homilist is prepared and focused. The homily will last ten to twelve minutes.

After the homily the catechumens (those desiring baptism at Easter) and the candidates (individuals seeking full communion at Easter) are dismissed so they can continue to study the Scripture readings for the day. The Creed is proclaimed. There are variations on the way the Creed is said at St. Patrick's.

Following the Creed is the general intercessions or the prayers of the faithful. The assembly may pray for the needs of the universal church, for national and world affairs, for the local community and the members of the assembly, for those who suffer physically or mentally, and for those who have died.

The people loudly and boldly respond, "Lord hear our prayer" to each petition. The prayers of the faithful concludes the first part of the mass, the Liturgy of the Word. The children return from their Liturgy of the Word, knowing in their hearts a little more about the love that Jesus has for them. All are seated.

Bread That Is Broken

The gifts of bread and wine are brought to the altar. The altar is prepared by the deacon, if present, or by the presider. The ministers of hospitality pass the collection baskets. Stewardship has been talked about in homilies at St. Patrick's for a number of years. Stewardship is based on Gospel values. The people give to the parish, not out of their excess, but as a willingness to give back to God who has so generously blessed them. Recently, the collection has gone up considerably because of this attitude of giving. St. Patrick's tithes are a percentage of their income. In seeking to be good stewards, the parish assists the poor and needy as well as a parish in a poorer socioeconomic area.

At this particular liturgy, the assembly sings during the preparation of the gifts. On some Sundays the choir may sing, or there may be an inspiring instrumental piece, or just silence.

The central prayer of the church begins:

The Lord be with you.

And also with you.

Lift up your hearts.

We lift them up to our Lord.

Let us give thanks to the Lord our God.

It is right to give him thanks and praise.

The dialogue between the presider and the assembly is stated clearly and strongly. The people are ready to participate fully in the eucharistic prayer through responding, singing, and active listening. The presider's gestures and response to the assembly welcomes full, active, and conscious participation by the people.

The assembly understands that the eucharistic prayer is the proclamation of God's saving work among his people, culminating in the life, death, and resurrection: the paschal mystery of Jesus Christ. It is at the altar that the assembly fully enters into the paschal mystery of Christ. The Holy Spirit transforms bread and wine into the Body and Blood of Christ. The bread and wine are not just a sign of Jesus; at the words of consecration, they become Jesus Christ. The assembly understands what a wonderful gift God has given to the church.

The eucharistic prayer concludes, and the presider chants, "Through him, with him and in him, in the unity of the Holy Spirit, all glory and honor is yours, almighty Father forever and ever. Amen." The assembly responds boldly to the eucharistic prayer with the singing of the Great Amen. It is a statement of belief that all that was proclaimed and done at the table of the Lord is true and holy.

For the singing of the Our Father, members of the assembly join hands in unity. People even reach across the aisle. The Lord's Prayer is usually sung at St. Patrick's, except during Lent. The greeting of peace is done with authenticity and respect. The assembly realizes the sign of peace is not a time to greet one another or say hello, but a time to look each other in the eye and offer Christ's peace. The people of St. Patrick's wish each other the peace of Christ through a firm handshake, an embrace, or a kiss.

The litany of the Lamb of God follows and it is sung. The eucharistic ministers gather around the altar. These extraordinary ministers of the eucharist represent a vast cross section of St. Patrick's from a teenager who was just confirmed, to a widowed grandmother, to a single father, to a newly married couple. They all have one thing in common, a deep love for the Eucharist and the church. The Body of Christ is distributed into communion bowls and the Blood of Christ is poured into cups.

"This is the Lamb of God who takes away the sins of the world; happy are those who are called to his supper." The people respond to this invitation to holy communion and the communion song begins. The music ministers have carefully chosen a song that the assembly knows very well. There is no need to carry a music book or song sheet. As the procession to receive the Eucharist begins, all of the assembly is singing a selection that reflects the sacred action that is taking place.

Although the communion procession keeps moving, each person is treated with dignity and respect. The eucharistic ministers look each person in the eye and prayerfully state, "The Body of Christ, the Blood of Christ." This action is never hurried, and the person has time to respond, "Amen." The minister then places the host in the hand or on the tongue, and hands over the chalice for the person to drink. Many members of the assembly partake of the Precious Blood.

In the past, instead of drinking from the communion cup, some members of the assembly would dip the host into the Blood of Christ. This practice is called intinction. This was done by people who were afraid of catching germs, but still wanted to receive the Blood of Christ. Through teaching and explanation, the assembly became aware that the practice of intinction is not part of the communion rite. The U.S. bishops have said that the Eucharist should never be dipped into the cup. Common sense and discretion is important when partaking of the communion cup. An individual who has a cold or other illness should refrain from drinking. The people have been informed that the Center for Disease Control has not recommended to the church that it abandon its custom of drinking the Blood of Christ from the communion cup. Jesus never said to take and dip, and the people of St. Patrick's take seriously the mandate from Christ to take and drink.

As a symbol of their service to the assembly, the music ministers share in communion last. The altar is cleared of the sacred vessels, the Blood of Christ is consumed and any extra consecrated bread is placed in the tabernacle for the sick, adoration, and reservation. Then there is silence.

It is a misconception that the liturgy, because it is public prayer, must always be filled with sound. The assembly has learned that silence plays an incredible role in the liturgy. The gift of silence prepares the heart to enter more fully into the paschal mystery of Christ at liturgy. The prayer after communion concludes the communion rite.

The Message Goes Forth

The final part of the liturgy concludes quickly. The parish announcements are read, the sending- forth song is announced, the assembly is blessed and challenged to love and serve the Lord and one another.

In the past individuals would begin to leave the liturgy as soon as communion started. That does not happen anymore at St. Patrick's. The assembly has learned that liturgy is a public ritual and all play an important role. It has taken a lot of work, but through time, prayer, education, and modeling, people now understand they have a vital function in the liturgy. All now stay and sing the entire sending-forth song. As the procession of the assembly makes its way back into the parking lot and automobiles, into neighborhoods and homes, and into schools and businesses, the work of the people at liturgy at St. Patrick's continues, as little by little they transform the world to Jesus Christ.

References

Archdiocese of Cincinnati Worship Office. *We Gather in Christ, Our Identity as Assembly.* Chicago: Liturgy Training Publications, 1996.

Bernadin, J. L. *Guide for the Assembly.* Chicago: Liturgy Training Publications, 1997.

Catholic Church. *General Instruction of the Roman Missal.* Chicago: Liturgy Training Publications, 1991.

Catholic Church. *Holy Communion and the Worship of the Eucharist Outside of Mass.* New York: Catholic Book Publishers, 1976.

Committee on the Liturgy, National Conference of Catholic Bishops. *Built of Living Stones: Art, Architecture, and Worship.* Washington, D.C.: U.S. Catholic Conference, 2000.

Committee on the Liturgy, National Conference of Catholic Bishops. *Environment and Art in Catholic Worship.* Chicago: Liturgy Training Publications, 1991.

Committee on the Liturgy, National Conference of Catholic Bishops. *Music in Catholic Worship*. Chicago: Liturgy Training Publications, 1991.

Gelineau, J. *Learning to Celebrate*. Washington, D.C.: Pastoral Press, 1985.

Horrigan, Phillip. "The Reconciliation Chapel." In *Clipnotes for Church Bulletins,* compiled and edited by Kathy Luty and David Philippart, 75. Vol. 1. Chicago: Liturgy Training Publications, 1997.

Mahony, R. M. *Gather Faithfully Together*. Chicago: Liturgy Training Publications, 1997.

Pope Pius XII. *Mediator Dei*. Rome: 1947.

Second Vatican Council. *Constitution on the Sacred Liturgy*. In *The Liturgy Documents*. 3rd ed. Vol. 1. Chicago: Liturgy Training Publications, 1991.